Geology Zone

# Gems

by Julie Murray

3

Dash!
LEVELED READERS
An Imprint of Abdo Zoom • abdobooks.com

**Level 1 – Beginning**
Short and simple sentences with familiar words or patterns for children who are beginning to understand how letters and sounds go together.

**Level 2 – Emerging**
Longer words and sentences with more complex language patterns for readers who are practicing common words and letter sounds.

**Level 3 – Transitional**
More developed language and vocabulary for readers who are becoming more independent.

**abdobooks.com**

Published by Abdo Zoom, a division of ABDO, PO Box 398166, Minneapolis, Minnesota 55439.


Printed in the United States of America, North Mankato, Minnesota.
102024
012025

Photo Credits: Getty Images, Shutterstock
Production Contributors: Kenny Abdo, Jennie Forsberg, Grace Hansen, John Hansen
Design Contributors: Candice Keimig, Neil Klinepier

**Library of Congress Control Number: 2024936539**

**Publisher's Cataloging in Publication Data**

Names: Murray, Julie, author.
Title: Gems / by Julie Murray
Description: Minneapolis, Minnesota : Abdo Zoom, 2025 | Series: Geology zone | Includes online resources and index.
Identifiers: ISBN 9781098287160 (lib. bdg.) | ISBN 9781098287863 (ebook) | ISBN 9781098288211 (Read-to-me ebook)
Subjects: LCSH: Gems--Juvenile literature. | Precious stones--Juvenile literature. | Rocks--Identification--Juvenile literature. | Geology--Juvenile literature. | Earth sciences--Juvenile literature.
Classification: DDC 553--dc23

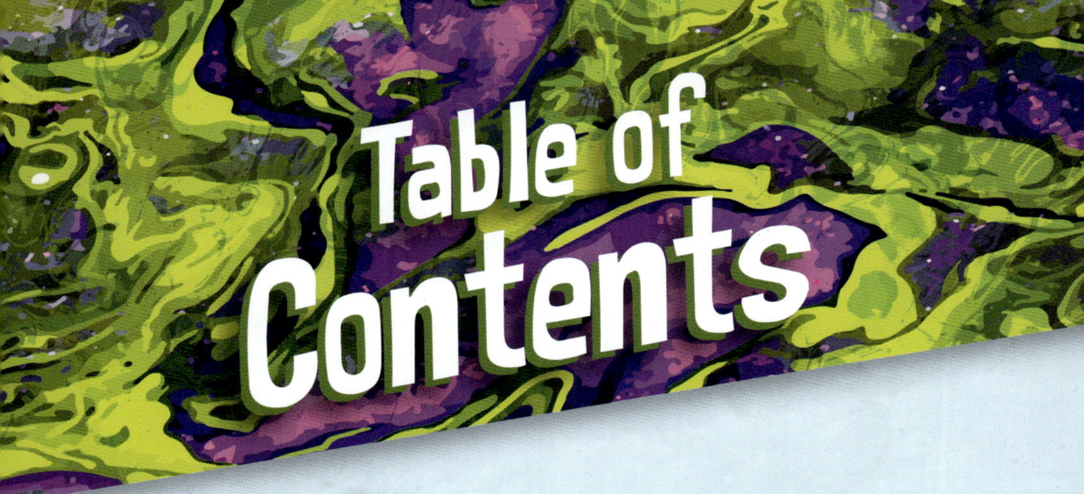

# Table of Contents

# Gems

Gems are beautiful, strong, and rare. Most come from **mineral crystals**. They form in rocks deep in the Earth.

# Crystal Systems

Cubic

Fluorite

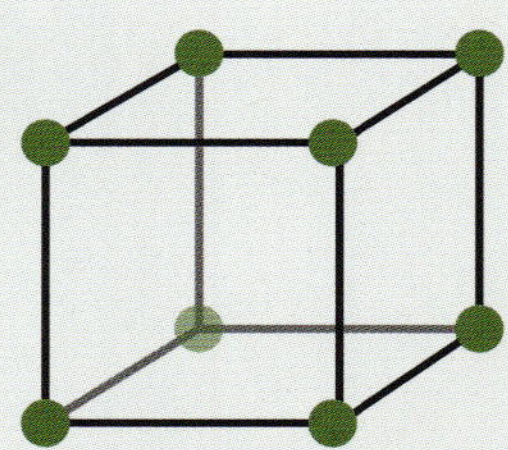

Tetragonal

Wulfenite

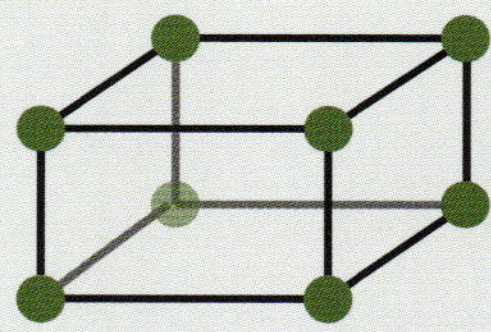

Orthorhombic

Tanzanite

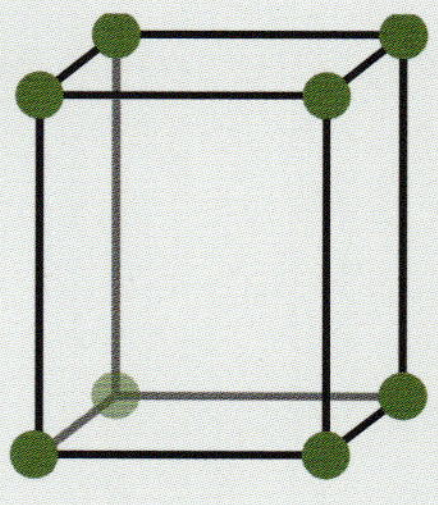

Monoclinic

Arurite

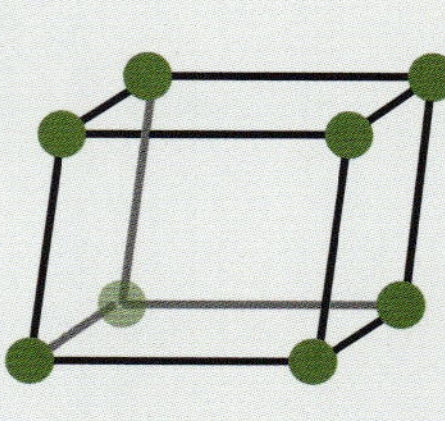

Each mineral is made up of different **atoms**. These atoms come together to form a crystal shape. Each crystal shape fits into one of the seven crystal systems.

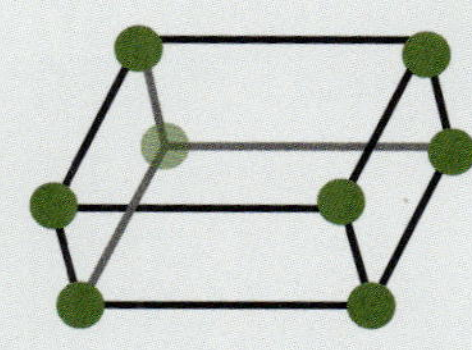

### Triclinic

Amazonite

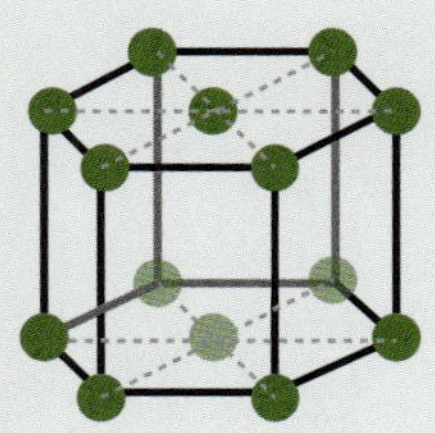

### Hexagonal

Emerald

### Trigonal

Rhodochrosite

Some gems form in magma. As the magma cools, crystals form. A ruby is formed this way.

## ROCK CYCLE

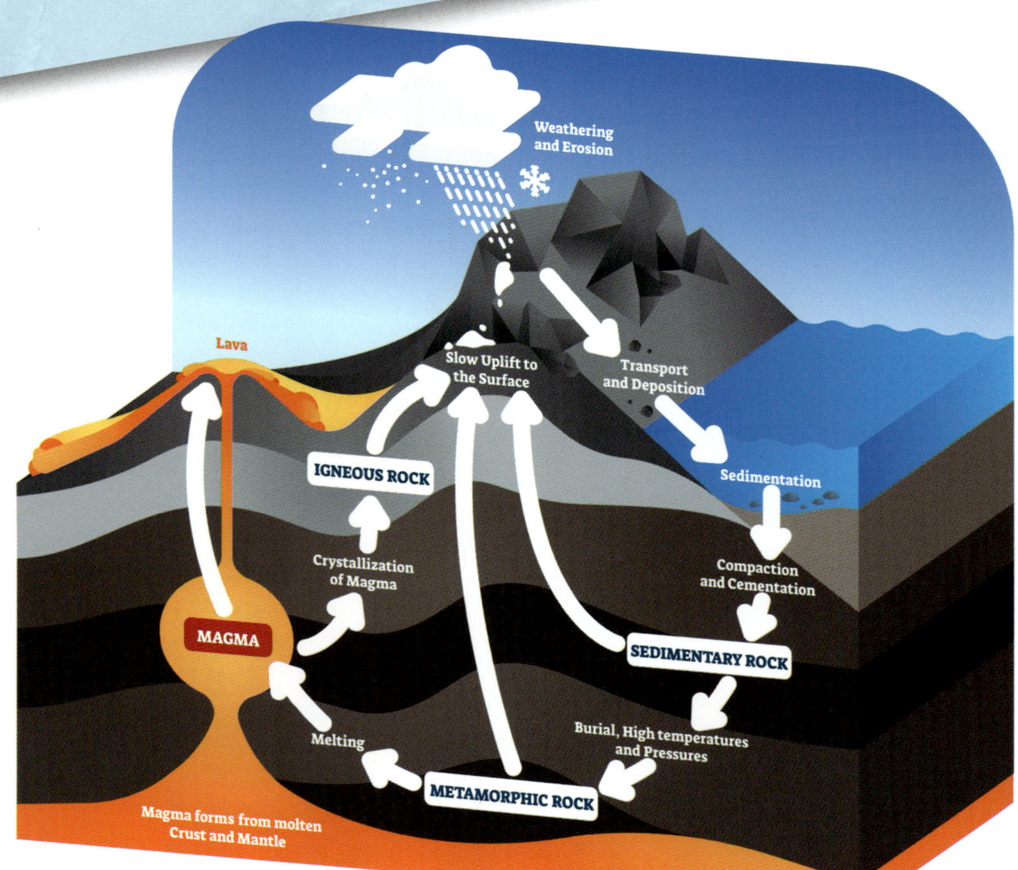

Some gems form as hot gases and fluids cool in the Earth. Topaz is formed this way.

Organic gems come from living or once living things. For example, an object, such as sand, can get into an oyster. Layers of **nacre** build up around the object. This is how pearls form!

# Precious vs. Semi-Precious

Gems are classified as being precious or semi-precious. This is based on their **rarity** and value. There are four precious gems. They are rubies, emeralds, sapphires and diamonds.

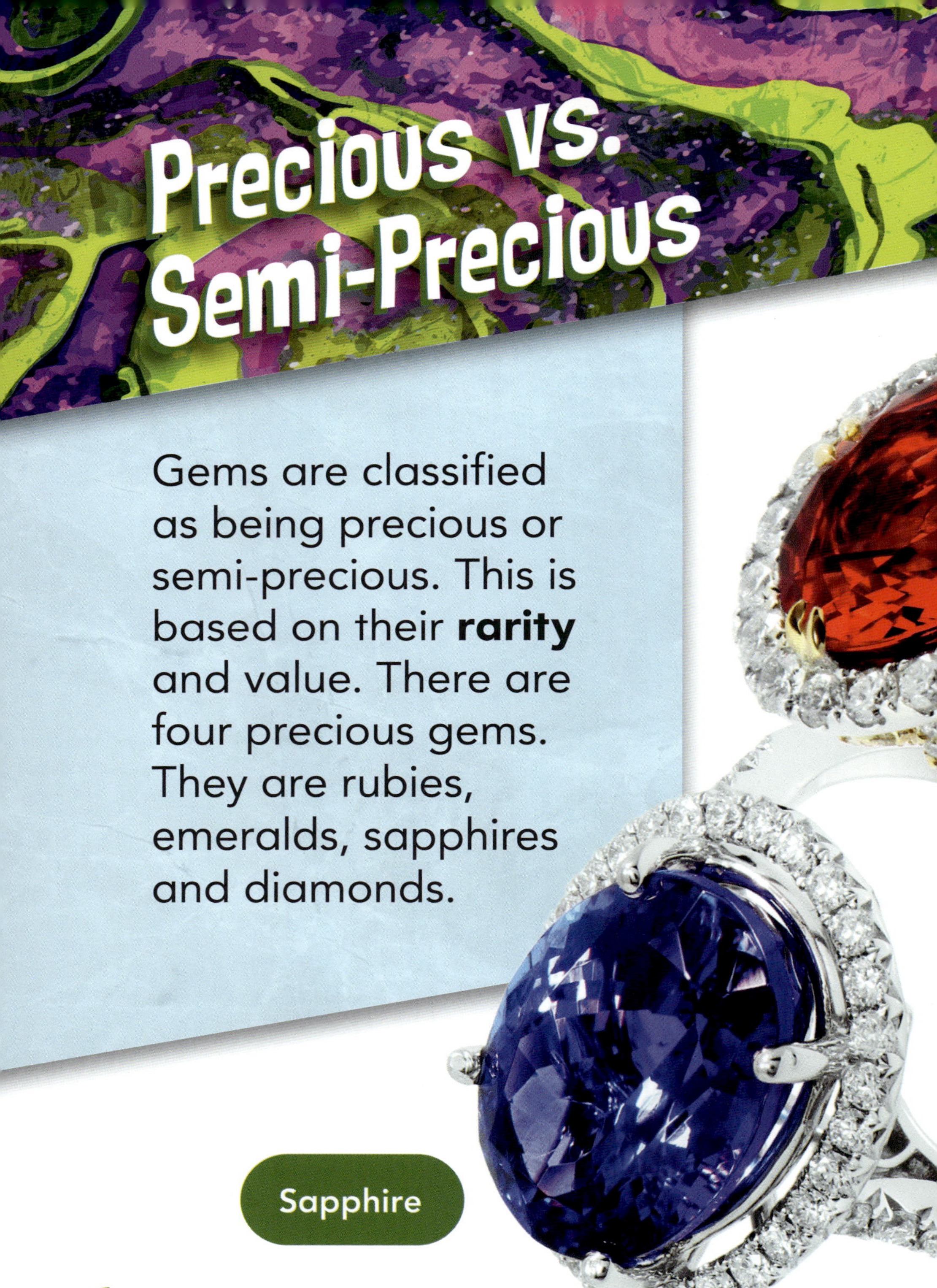

Sapphire

Ruby
Emerald

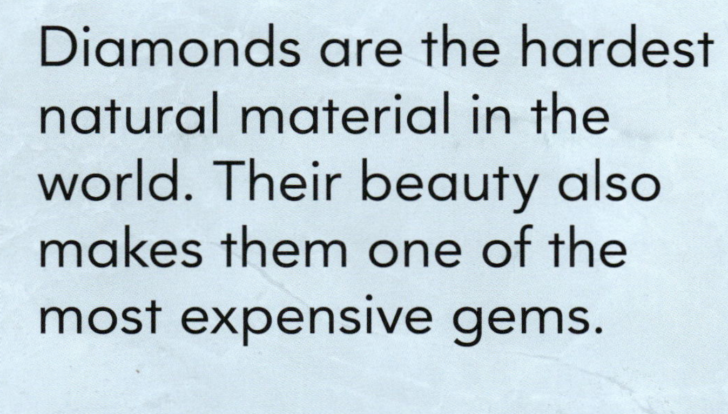

Diamonds are the hardest natural material in the world. Their beauty also makes them one of the most expensive gems.

Other gems are considered semi-precious. They come in a variety of colors. **Amethysts** and **garnets** are some popular ones.

Amethyst

Garnet

# How Are Gems Used?

JAN
Garnet

FEB
Amethyst

MAR
Aquamarine

APR
Diamond

MAY
Emerald

JUNE
Moonstone

JULY
Ruby

AUG
Peridot

SEPT
Sapphire

OCT
Pink Tourmaline

NOV
Citrine

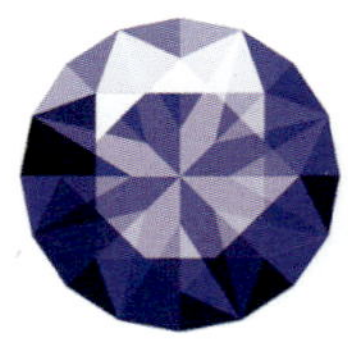

DEC
Tanzanite

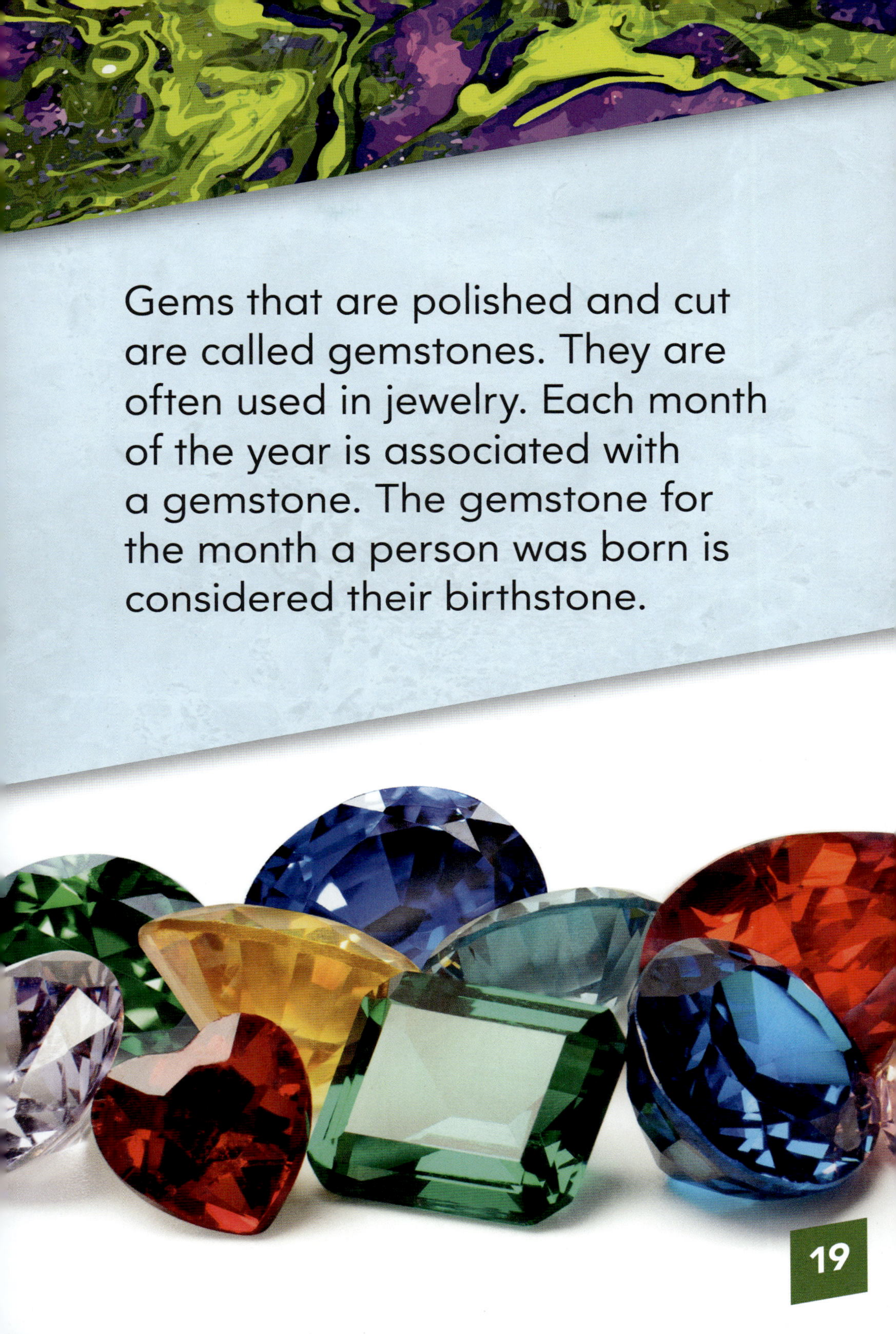

Gems that are polished and cut are called gemstones. They are often used in jewelry. Each month of the year is associated with a gemstone. The gemstone for the month a person was born is considered their birthstone.

Some people believe that gemstones have healing properties. Clear quartz is used for energy. It is said to balance the mind and body.

**Amethyst** is said to help take away sadness and irritability.

# More Facts

- Most gems form 3 to 25 miles (4.8 to 40 km) below the Earth's surface. Diamonds form deeper than 125 miles (201 km) in the Earth.
- Diamonds can take anywhere from 1 to 3 billion years to form!
- Gemstones have four important factors known as the "Four Cs." They are cut, color, clarity, and carat.

# Glossary

**amethyst** – a clear purple or bluish-violet variety of crystallized quartz that is often used in jewelry.

**atom** – the smallest possible unit of a chemical element.

**garnet** – a common type of hard mineral that can have a variety of colors and includes the dark red stone often used in jewelry.

**mineral crystal** – a crystalline form of a chemical compound.

**nacre** – a hard, iridescent material lining certain seashells.

**rarity** – condition of being rare or unusual.

# Index



# Online Resources

To learn more about gems, please visit **abdobooklinks.com** or scan this QR code. These links are routinely monitored and updated to provide the most current information available.